Souvenir roc

Written by Noreen Wetton and Jenny McWhirter

Illustrated by Hemesh Alles

Nelson

"Just a minute, you two," said Mum from inside the caravan.
"Where are you off to? You know we have to be off the site by
midday. And there's all this packing up to do."

Lenny and Rose looked at each other. They loved caravan
holidays, especially when they travelled round stopping at
new places, meeting new people. The only thing they hated
was the packing up. Everything had to be put away in the
right place. And Mum always seemed to get short tempered
at packing up time.

"Can't we go down to the beach just for a last look before we have to go?" asked Rose.

"It's our favourite place," said Lenny. "And I want to say goodbye to it."

"Well," said Mum. "I suppose so. You aren't much help here. But don't go out of sight, and don't get dirty, and don't . . ."

"OK Mum," said Rose and Lenny together and ran off before Mum could finish her sentence.

In and out of the caravans they ran, through the gate by the little shop which never closed, and down the path to the beach.

"Let's go to our special place," said Rose. "The one with all the pebbles and stones and bits of rock. We can choose some to add to our collection."

"We've got fifteen already," said Lenny. "And the box is nearly full. My favourite is the big pebble with the fossil in it."

They walked along slowly, looking down, scuffling their feet, and now and then stopping to pick up a pebble that seemed specially smooth or shiny or a funny shape.

Then Rose stopped. She looked, and looked again. In the track she had made with her feet she could see something shiny. She bent down, picked it up, and put it into the palm of her hand. It was a rough piece of gold.

Very carefully she turned it round and round, then turned it over. Whichever way she looked at it, it was still a lump of gold. Nothing else. No streaks of black or any other colour. Just gold.
She stood quite still, watching the way it gleamed in the bright sunshine.

"Lenny," she said. Her voice was quite croaky. "Lenny, come and look at this." Lenny turned round and ran back. "What've you found? Is it a –" and then he stopped. He looked and looked.

"Where did you get that?" he asked. "It looks like – like gold!" "It is, I think," said Rose. "I found it under my feet."

"What are we going to do with it?" asked Lenny. "Are we going to put it in our collection?"

"Yes," said Rose. "And you're not to tell anyone. When we get back home we'll take it down to Big Ben at the rock shop, and . . ." Rose and Lenny looked at each other. They didn't dare finish the sentence. Perhaps . . . was all they could think.

The journey home seemed very long. Lenny and Rose sat in the back with their books and games and their collection box. Now and then one of them would lift the lid of the box and peep inside just to check that the gold was still there.

"What are you two whispering about?" asked Mum without turning round.
"Nothing Mum," said Rose and Lenny together.

It was too late when they got home to go and show their pebbles and stones and bits of rock to Big Ben. Rose put the collection box on the table at the side of her bed. But Lenny took out the gold, wrapped it in an old sock and slept with it under his pillow.

Next morning they rushed off out of the house to Big Ben's
Rock Shop in the market square. They took with them the
gold, the pebble with the fossil in it, and small egg-shaped
rocks which they had found on a hillside at the start of their
holiday.

There were lots of people in the shop as usual, sorting
through the polished pebbles and stones Big Ben had set out
in baskets on the counter.

"Ben", said Rose. "Ben, can we talk to you? It's very important."

"Wait five minutes," said Ben. "Then I'm going to stop for a cup of tea, and we can talk."

The five minutes seemed like five hours but at last Ben came out from behind the counter.

"What have you got to show me this time?" he said. "Any fossils?" Carefully Rose and Lenny unwrapped the fossil pebble, the two small egg-shaped rocks, and . . . the gold.

Ben sat down on an old box, looked at the pebble, the rocks, and the gold and said:

"Well now. You've got one that isn't all that valuable, but it's interesting because it's a fossil."

"And . . . ?", whispered Rose, hopping with excitement.

"And two that could be quite valuable if we can look inside."

"Two!" said Lenny. "But there's only *one* piece of gold."

"Wait a minute." said Ben. "I haven't finished. The one that looks like gold isn't gold at all. In fact it's called fool's gold."

"Fool's gold!" said Rose and Lenny together.

"Fooled you, did it?" said Ben. "Never mind. It fools lots of people. Real gold doesn't look like that at all. But let's look inside one of these. They don't look very exciting but you might be lucky."

He went over to his saw. He switched it on and very carefully he sawed one of the egg-shaped rocks in half. "No, nothing there," he said. "Let's try the other one."

This time, as the two halves came apart Lenny and Rose could see the dark purple colour of amethyst.

"Well, well, well," said Ben. "That's one of the best I've seen. You've found a real treasure. Take it home and show your Mum. Tell her that if she wants I can sell it for you."

Rose and Lenny walked back up the hill to their house.

"Fool's gold!"said Rose. "It fooled us, didn't it!"

"The outside fooled us," said Lenny. "And so did the other rock. The outside looked ordinary, but inside it was valuable and beautiful."

"I don't think I like being fooled," said Rose. "I'm going to ask Mum if we can borrow a book from the library and find out how you can tell about rocks."

"Good idea," said Lenny. "But first let's try out our fool's gold on Mum. Perhaps it will fool her too."